Amatsu-tatara hisshin-ginkoroku Kangi no maki

天津韛韜謐心闇諱録槙技之巻

Hanbo Jutsu

Transcription & Illustrations by Kazuhiro Iida

Translated by Eric Shahan

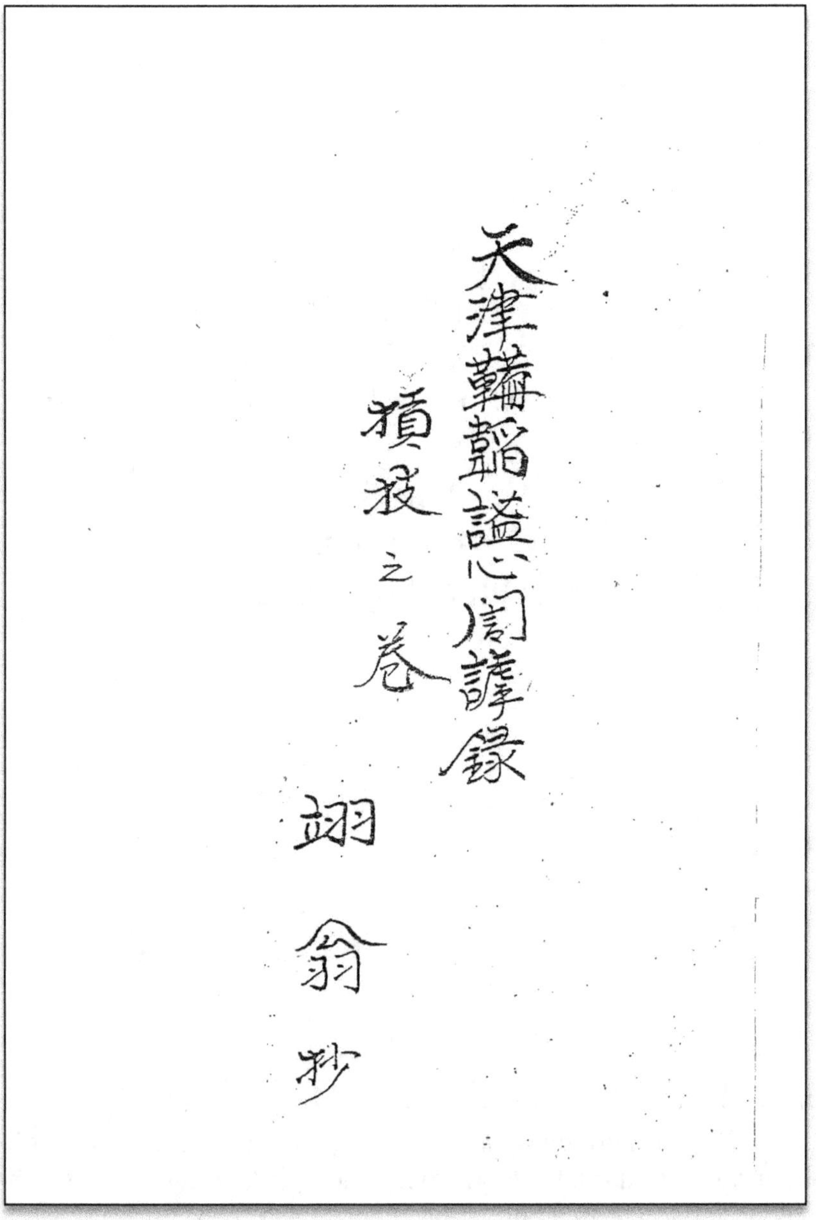

「天<ruby>津<rt>あ</rt></ruby>輴韜謐心闇譿録　槓技之巻」
（※読み方は不確かです。）
Amatsu-tatara hisshin-ginkoroku Kangi no maki[1]

翊翁抄
Yokuou shou
A Document by Yokuou[2]

---

[1] *Amatsu-tatara hisshin*-ginkoroku is a series of more than 20 scrolls about various martial arts, medical and spiritual matters from the Kuki Family. This reading of the characters is approximate since no reading is given. *Kangi no Maki* means Kangi scroll, it is not clear what "Kangi" means.

[2] This is a used by Takamatsu Toshitsugu 高松寿嗣 (1889~ 1972.)

半棒術解説

此半棒と云ふ云葉を現在は杖術と称して居る人もある最

古に於ては之を刀棒之法と古止文に残されている

恐らく武器としては此半棒が最も最古であらう一説流の一

説に根の国の野系で素盞嗚尊が大国主を試す為め四方

の枯草に火をつけ野系の草付思ち火となった時に大国主命

は一本橋を拾って此火を凪ぎ倒し防がれた處へ一足の鼠が来

て命を救ったことを又古止文に云雲武命が三尺の棒刀を以て敵を

退治したことを見ても確に古い武器だと云ふ事が判りますが

此の武器を使ふ法と積技之巻半棒と云ふのであります凡て武

道と云ふず宗門的妙術で進しも修行中に必ず経験する

事と思ふが進歩は必ずしも同じ速度で行ゝものではないのです

半棒術解説

此半棒と云ふ業を現在は杖術と称しておる人もある。最古に於ては之を刀棒之法と古止文に残されている。恐らく武器としては此半棒が最も最古であったらしい。説話の一説に根の国（日本神話に出てくる異界）の野原で素盞鳴（すさのおの）尊（みこと）（一般的には素盞鳴尊）が大国主を滅す為め四方の枯草に火をつけ、野原の草は忽ち火となった時に大国主命は一本棒を拾って此火を凪ぎ倒し防がれた處（ところ）へ一疋の鼠が来て命を救ったこと又古止文に出雲武命が三尺の棒刀を以て敵を退治したこと（※『古事記』『日本書紀』等と比べて内容がかなり相違している。）を見ても確に古武器だと云ふのであります。凡そ武道と云はず宗門的妙術でも誰しも修行中に必ず経験する事と思ふが進歩は必ずとも同じ

半棒術解説
Hanbo Jutsu Kaisetsu
An Exclamation of Hanbo Jutsu

Though Hanbo techniques use a half-staff measuring 3 Shaku 90 centimeters, many people today refer to these techniques as Jojutsu, referring to the 4 Shaku 120 centimeter police staff. The oldest references can be found in ancient documents that refer to it as part of a "Sword and Stick Method."

As far as weapons go, the Hanbo is probably the oldest weapon. It is talked about in legends from the Root Domain, a mysterious realm mentioned in Japanese tales. Susano Ono Mikoto, the younger brother of the goddess of the sun, Amaterasu, was in a field in the Root Domain. He sought to kill the king of a powerful domain by lighting the dry grasses on all sides of the field on fire.

The flames roared to life and the whole field was set ablaze. However a mouse was able to find a staff of wood and he brought this to the great king who used this to sweep the flames aside and escape.[3]

Also there are ancient documents that record Izumo Takeru using a 3 Shaku, 90 centimeter, staff of wood as if it were a sword to force his enemies to retreat. Therefore we can confirm that this weapon indeed comes to us from the distant past.

People often find that as they train martial arts, there are times when the techniques are religious or spiritual in nature. Even if they start at the same time, two people will never progress at the same speed.

---

[3] This story is mentioned in both the Kojiki and the Nihonshoki, both written in the 8th century, however the details are quite different. The section in question from the Kojiki has been included at the end of this book.

或る時期には吾れ等の不思議と思ふ程の進歩を見る事があるか
或場合は丸で反対でそれの身体は死物同様如何に努力しも
あせってもナしも思ふ様に働くことが出来なくなる事がある
それは多々一つの惰性から更に上に上る時期に起る現象で例
へば技丈けで満足出来なくなり精神的方面を重んじて来る
称な時期等の如き技の精神を重んずる今り技の実際と精神
との調和がとれず今度に刺ほ技が刺かなくなったりする。之は
修行途上の最も重大な一時期である。こうなると丸で技も出来
体も刺がなくなった、いくら替えてし不思議に身体が動かず
自分の思ふ様な技が出来ないと悲観してて中止する者がある
又宗門の妙術も少うし刺がなくなって悲観の余り進む已
れでけされ以上進歩はけないのだと思う信仰もー分くなる時

或る時期には吾れ乍ら不思議と思ふ程の進歩を見る事があるが、或場合は丸で反対で己れの身体は死物同様、如何に努力してもあせっても少しも思ふ様に働くことが出来なくなる事がある。それは多々一つの階段から更に上に上がる時期に起る現象で例へば技丈けで満足出来なくなり精神的方面を重んじて来る様な時期等の如々技の精神を重んずる余り技の実際と精神との調和がとれず今迄に利いた技が利かなくなったりする。之は修行途上の最も重大な一時期である。こをなると丸で技も出ない体も利かなくなった。いくら稽古しても不思議に身体が動かず自分の思ふ様な技が出来ないと悲観して了ひ中止する者がある。又、宗門の妙術も少こしも利かなくなって悲観のあまり迎も己では、これ以上進歩はしないのだと思って信仰もしなくなる時

There will be times when you will be startled to find your skills are improving faster than expected. Other times it will be the exact opposite. It will feel as if your body is dead and matter how much effort you put in, you cannot seem to match the movement you are aiming for. However, be aware that this phenomenon likely occurs when you are close to attaining the next level in your martial arts.

This could be happening because you are unconsciously becoming dissatisfied with the breadth of your technique. When such a period in your life occurs, your state of mind is reflected in the techniques you are using. Your mind and the technique you are employing are not unified. This means that techniques that you were previously able to employ effectively, have now become ineffective. In fact, this is the most important point in your martial arts training. It is when your body becomes wholly unable to execute techniques, your movement becomes poor and your timing is off.

No matter how much you train, quite mysteriously your body will not move and you will not be able to execute techniques in the manner you had heretofore been able to. Some people who enter this stage are so disappointed that they quit training. Further, you will be saddened to realize you are completely unable to execute the more esoteric techniques. This leads to a period where you lose faith and feel your martial arts will no longer progress beyond this point.

期が来る又法だとか霊感だとか云ふものを疑ひたくなる事そこで
迷ふ心が出る法とか霊感と云ふ前に諸君はいろは四十八文
字の内に（う）と云ふ字ゎ四十八文字の内の何番目にあるかと
尋ねると誰れでもが始めからいろはと云ふて見なくては判らない
でせう又一七八九の数を三で割つて見よと云ふと諸君は直ぐ三
一三一と割算の九々の計算をするでせう之は何ンず型でせう
此型を会得すればこそ出来るのでせう之です此型の練習に精神が
悟り得て始め完成するのです故何ンと人間ては出来ないのは
必ず出来る稽古を忠けては駄目です之が練習中に必ずある現
象でかゝる場合何んくそ鉄を貫く貫徹心を起す事です
私ゎ修養中一人の主席の柔道家を倒す事た日夜考へて
三ケ月目に妖つて倒するのが出来ました又天名宗僧門に有る時

期が来る。又、法だとか霊感だとか云ふものを疑ひたくなる。そこで迷ふ心が出る。法とか霊感を疑ふ前に諸君は、いろは四十八文字の内に（う）と云ふ字わ四十八文字の内の何書目にあるかと尋ねると誰れでもが始めから、いろはと云ふて見なくては判らないでせう。又、一七八九の数を三で割って見よと云ふと諸君は直ぐ三一、三一と割算の九々の計算をするでせう。之は何です。型でせう。此型を会得すればこそ出来るのでせう。之です。此型の練習に精神が悟り得て始めて完成するのです。故、何でも人間には出来ない事はない。必ず出来る。　稽古を怠けては駄目です。之が練習中に必ずある現象でかゝる場合、何くそ鉄をも貫く貫徹心を起す事です。私は修養中、一人の上席の柔道家を倒す事に日夜考へて三ケ月目に始めて倒す事が出来ました。又、天台宗僧門に有る時

This causes people to begin to doubt what we call "this method" or what we call "divine inspiration." This is the source of doubt. For those of you doubting this technique or divine inspiration, I ask you to consider the following:

If I were to ask where the letter "U" falls on the Japanese alphabet, everyone would begin by chanting I, Ro, Ha…without that rhyme, no one would know how to determine where that letter falls. Further, if I were to ask you to divide 1789 by 3, most everyone would being by going 3-1,3-1 while using 9 X 9 division.

So, what am I taking about here? This is Kata, techniques.

If you learn the techniques described in this book you will become proficient. This is the point I am making.

Train these techniques until your spirit begins to revel their inner secrets and mysteries to you. Then you will have achieved mastery, and your training will be complete.

Thus, there is nothing you cannot accomplish. You will invariably succeed, however you cannot neglect your training.

This phenomenon will invariably occur during training. When it does happen, the realization will strike you as if you have been impaled by a steel bar. In the early days of my training there was a senior Judo practitioner I wished to defeat. I pondered day and night for three months what strategy I could use to defeat him. After that I defeated him for the first time.

京都の警察から犯人を捜査する為に聞きに来た私は三十分間に於て犯人の身長歳頃逃走を明確に的中さしたが此霊感を得る迄に山中の辯天之堂に於て毎朝三時から寒中尺の雪をふいで精神の統一を修行った事二ケ年です或時は絶食三週間病人に施す法を以て十手からの全身ふづい者を救った事とも今色も萬事に貫く精神こそ所安であります

一筋に貫く心　極意ぞと
たゆまず学べ神の教を

翔　翁

京都の警察から犯人を捜査する為に聞きにこられた私は三十分間に於て犯人の身長、歳頃（年頃）、逃走先を明確に的中さしましたが此霊感を得る迄に山中の辨天堂に於て毎朝三時から寒中、尺の雪をふいで精神の統一を修行した事、一ヶ年です。或時は絶食二週間病人に虎ノ法を以って十年からの全身ふづい者を救ったこともあり、兎も角萬事に貫く精神こそ肝要であります。

　　一筋に貫く心　極意ぞと
　　たゆまず学べ神の教を
　　　　　　　　　翊翁

When I was serving as a monk at Tendai Temple in Kyoto, the police came to me for assistance in locating a criminal. Within 30 minutes I had accurately determined the criminal's height, age and the place where he fled. However, in order to attain this level of spiritual awareness I had to live in the mountains. I stayed at a temple called the Hall of Benten. I would rise at 3 am every morning and train (mediate) in the deep snow. I spent one year doing this training in order to unify my body and spirit.

I once used the Tora no Ho, Tiger Method, to help a sick person who had been rendered unable to eat for two weeks. Though he had been paralyzed for ten years, I was able to heal him. Thus, forging the mind so that it can overcome any situation is essential.

A straight line that pierces through the spirit.
The ultimate is an unceasing study of diving teachings

Yokuoh

解説

半棒は痛無き構と云ふのであります
争ふ武器ではない、のであります即ち武器を以て構へず心の構として
でありますが半棒術として
完成したのは延元三年正月足利尊氏京都に大軍を以て押寄
せた時官軍の結城親光の従者大国を御武者足利方の
此勢に當る可からざるを大国を前槍を以て立向ける
剛傑八代権之守氏郷三尺八寸の軍刀にて味方に切込む
急ち八代氏郷の為めに槍の真中より真二つに切折られたり
大国を訊手に残りたる槍の柄三尺にて飛込みまま八代氏郷を
一撃り之に剣し刀を抜って其面を揚げたりより半棒術
の完成としたるに有り古止之文一片の為一也

心　え

心　え　構

解説

半棒は構無き構と云ふのでありまして劒の如く敵と対抗して爭ふ武器ではないのであります。即ち武器を以て構へず、心の構であります。　此半棒は最古の武器ではありますが、半棒術として完成したのは延元三年正月、足利尊氏、京都に大軍を以て押寄せたと時、官軍の結城親光の従者、大国太郎武秀、足利方の豪傑、八代權之守氏郷、三尺八寸の軍刀にて味方に切込む。　此勢い、当る可からざるを大国太郎、槍を以て立向いけるに忽ち八代氏郷の為めに槍の真中より真二つに切折られたり。　大国太郎、手に残りたる槍の柄三尺にて飛込みさま、八代氏郷を一撃の元に倒し、刀を拔いて其首を揚げたり。之より半棒術の完成となりたるに有り。　古止文一片の寫し也。

心之構

Explanation

Hanbo uses a "Kamae of no Kamae," or a "Stance of no Stance." This means the way you stand at the beginning of techniques is characterized by the lack of a basic stance. However, the Hanbo is not intended to be used like a sword and battle against people. What this means is you don't go into a stance holding this weapon, rather you position yourself with a certain state of mind.

While the Hanbo is the oldest weapon in the world, Hanbo Jutsu, the art of using the half-staff wasn't completely formed until the 3rd year of Engen (1336,) when Ashikaga Takauji was advancing on Kyoto with his huge army. One group of the defenders was commanded by Yuki Chikamitsu. He had a Samurai named Taikoku Taro Takahide under his command.

Ashikaga and his master swordsman Hachiyo Guardian of Gon Ujisato began their advance. The Samurai Hachiyo was relentless in his advance, cutting into the defenders with his 3 Shaku 8 Sun, or 1.2-meter, military sword.

Taikoku Taro, realizing he could not stand against such a ferocious onslaught, grabbed a spear and met Hachiyo in combat. However, Hachiyo's first attack neatly cut Taikoku's spear in half. Taikoku Taro picked up the remaining 3 Shaku, 90-centimeter, end of his spear, the part without a sword tip, and charged Hachiyo, knocking him down with one blow. He then drew his Katana and cut off Hachiyo's head, before raising it high. This is how Hanbo fighting came to be. This tale was copied from a fragment of an old document.

一、型破構無構

之は棒の両端五寸内を持って両面に両手落したる也

一文字の如くと云ふ

一、無心構無構

之は右の手に棒状に突きたる姿の構

一、音無構無構

之は型破形の反対に棒の両端五寸内を両手に以て棒は後ろに持ちたる女の構

之を三心の備もと云ふ也

一、型破構無構

之は棒の両端五寸内を持って正面に両手落したる

平一文字の如くを云ふ

一、無心構無構

之は右の手に棒、杖に突きたる姿の構

一、音無構無構

之は型破形の反対に棒の両端五寸内を両手に

以て棒は後ろに持ちたる姿の構

之を三心の溝とも云ふ丗

- *Kata Yaburi Kamae Mu Kamae[4]*
  Breaking the Technique Stance, No-stance

Face your Attacker while holding the Hanbo with both hands about 5 Sun, 15 centimeters, from each end. Both hands should hang naturally, like Hira Ichi Monji, or Standing Open Like the Kanji for One 一.

---

[4] There were no illustrations in this manual, these are all done by Kazuhiro Iida and are for reference.

- *Mushin Kamae Mu Kamae*
  Without Mind, No-stance

Hold one end of the Hanbo in your right hand with the other end on the ground. This stance looks like you are standing with a walking stick.

- *Otonashi Mu Kamae*
  Without Sound, No-stance

This stance is the opposite of Breaking the Technique stance. Your hands hold the Hanbo 5 Sun, 15 centimeters from each end, but it is behind your back.

These stances are called the Sanshin, "three hearts" or three states of mind.

一、型破構無構

之は棒の両端五寸内を持ちて正面に両手落したる
一文字の如くそろふ

一、無心構無構

之は右の手に棒状に突きたる姿の構
之は型破形の反対に棒の両端五寸内を両手に
以て棒は後ろに持ちたる女の構

之を三心の構とも云ふ也

初段 無心構無構
相手方片手にて我片胸襟を捕りて右手小刀にて突き来る
片手折、我左足一歩引き体を左斜めにして同じに敵の
左手左側に高く上げて同じに敵の左腕の中関節を棒
中真にて突き折る

突落 相手方前と今じく左手ノ片約右手小刀突へり来る
我前の一文字の棒其まゝ、敵の左腕中関節にて突入る
のと左足引き一寸腰をかゞめるのを同じ忽ち左手ノ放ちて

一、型破構無構

之は棒の両端五寸内を持って正面に両手落したる
平一文字の如くを云ふ

一、無心構無構

之は右の手に棒、杖に突きたる姿の構

一、音無構無構

之は型破形の反対に棒の両端五寸内を両手に以
て棒は後ろに持ちたる姿の構　之を三心の構とも云ふ也

片手折

相手方、片手にて我片胸襟を捕りて右手小刀にて突き来る。

初段※無心構無構　※型破構無構の間違い

突落

相手方、前と仝じく左手片胸右手小刀突入り来る。
我、左足一歩引き体を左斜めにして右手をそのま、敵の左
手左側に高く出して同じ（同時）に敵の左腕の中関節を棒
中真にて突き折る。

Shodan
Initial Level
All Kata in this section are from Without Mind, No-stance

- *Mushin Kamae Mu Kamae*
  Without Mind, No-stance

Kata-te Ori
One-handed Break

Your Attacker has a short sword in his right hand. He seizes your lapel with his left hand and stabs, aiming for your stomach.
Respond by stepping back with your left foot so your body is angled away from the Attacker. Keeping your hands in the same position thrust your Hanbo up towards the left side of the Attacker's left arm. By doing this the center of the Hanbo should strike the Attacker directly in the elbow, breaking it.

Tsuki Otoshi
Stab and Drop

Your Attacker stabs the same way as before. He grabs your left lapel with one hand and, with a short sword in his right hand, tries to stab you in the stomach.

You respond by staying in Ichimonji Kamae, with your body straight like the Kanji for One 一, as you step back with your left foot, dropping your hips slightly. At the same time, use both hands to shove your Hanbo up, striking the Attacker in the elbow of his left arm with the center of your Hanbo. Then immediately use your left hand to fling the left end of the Hanbo toward the Attacker's head. As you swing the Hanbo with your right hand, join your left hand on the end so you are holding the right end with both hands as you strike the Attacker in the face with the right end of the Hanbo.

左棒先敵の顔面に突入り

打技

我れ体を一歩左足左横へ〜て体を転じ左手持ち左棒先

敵の小手打込み甚ま、左横面サ入る

相手方小刀にて我腹部を突入り来る

流補

相手方前と同じく小刀にて我れが腹部に突入り来る我右足

右横へ一歩開き体を転じ左手にて敵の小刀持ち右手西

を握り右棒先を敵の後ろ腰に持て行き右手と敵の

右腕付根に持って行き左足と右後ろ斜めに持つ

行くと敵の右腕が棒の為と左手にて手西を持って

いる為に逆になる、敵仰向けた倒れる棒尻で脇つぼ

当込む

左棒先敵の顔面に突入り。

打技

相手方、小刀にて我腹部を突入り来る。

我れ体を一歩左足左横へして体を転じ左手放ち左棒先敵の小手打込み其まゝ、左横面打入る。

流捕

相手方、前と全じく小刀にて我れが腹部に突入り来る。我、右足右横へ一歩開き体を転じ左手にて敵の小刀持つ右手首を握り右法先を敵の後ろ腰に持て行き、右手を敵の右腕付根に持って行き左足を右後ろ斜めに持って行くと敵の右腕が棒の為と左手にて手首を持っている為に逆になる。敵卯句けに到れる。棒尤で脇つぼ当込む。

Uchi Waza
Striking Technique

Your Attacker attacks by trying to stab you in the stomach with his short sword.[5]

____

[5] Uchi Waza (Illustrations interpreted from the text.) Step 1.

You respond by stepping to the left with your left foot allowing your body to rotate clockwise. Release the Hanbo with your left hand and swing it with your right so you strike your Attacker's wrists with the left end of your Hanbo.[6]

---

[6] Step 2: Step back and to the left with your left foot. Avoid the opponent's stab with his short sword by throwing the (A) end of the Hanbo to strike him in the right wrist.

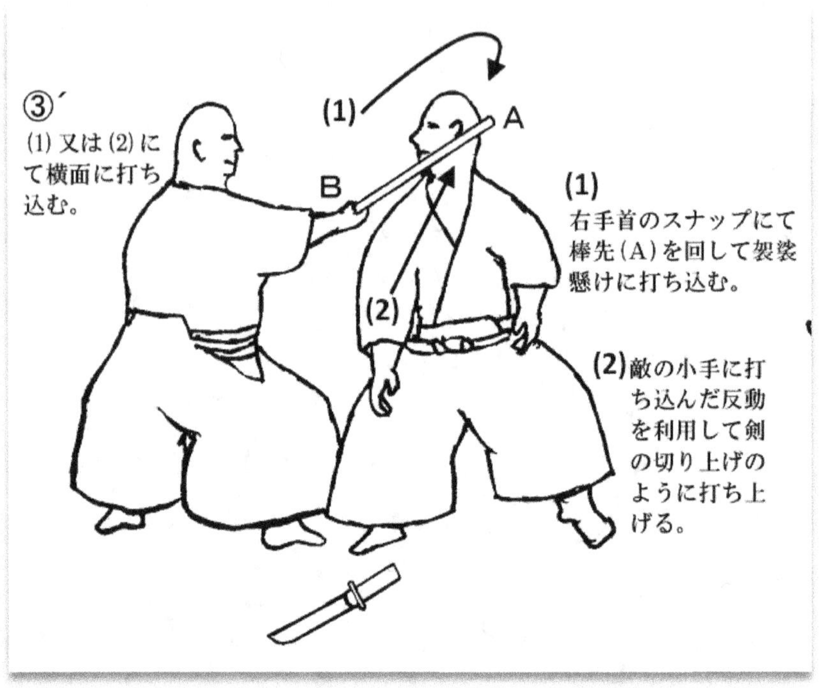

Then, from that position, strike the left side of his face.[7]

---

[7] Step 3:

The Yokomen, strike to the side · of the head, can be to either point (1) or (2).

1. Use the snap of your right wrist to strike Kesa. Kesa is a diagonal downward cutting motion, as if you were cutting down a monk's vestment.

2. After striking the wrist, you can rebound from that and strike upward to the head like with a sword.

Original Version

1. Your Attacker attacks by trying to stab you in the stomach with his short sword

2. Step back and to the left with your left foot. Avoid the opponent's stab with his short sword by throwing the (A) end of the Hanbo to strike him in the right wrist.

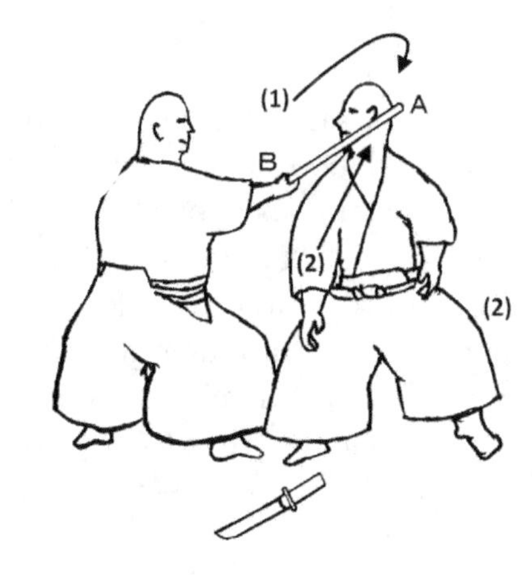

3. As you step forward with your left foot, swing the left end of the Hanbo directly into the Attacker's face.

Alternate Final Strike 1

1. Your Attacker attacks by trying to stab you in the stomach with his short sword

2. Step back and to the left with your left foot. Avoid the opponent's stab with his short sword by throwing the (A) end of the Hanbo to strike him in the right wrist.

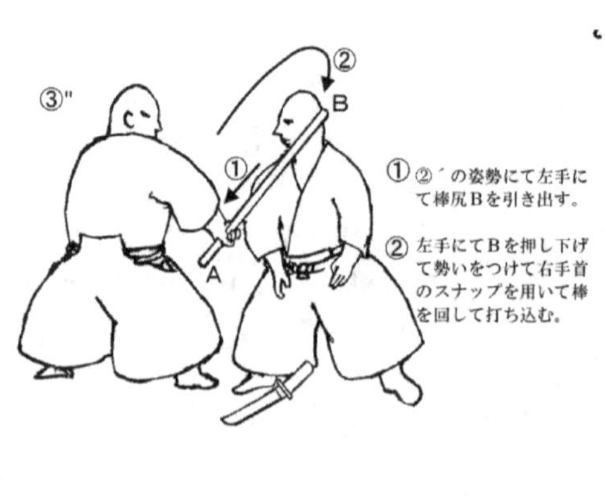

From the position in step 2, grab point (B) of the Hanbo with your left hand. Use your left hand to push the Hanbo down, accelerating it. Release and use your right wrist to continue the motion, snapping it into the side of the Attacker's head with (B.)

Alternate Final Strike 2

1. Your Attacker attacks by trying to stab you in the stomach with his short sword

2. Step back and to the left with your left foot. Avoid the opponent's stab with his short sword by throwing the (A) end of the Hanbo to strike him in the right wrist.

3. As you step forward with your left foot, swing the left end of the Hanbo directly into the Attacker's face.

Nagare Dori
Flowing Capture

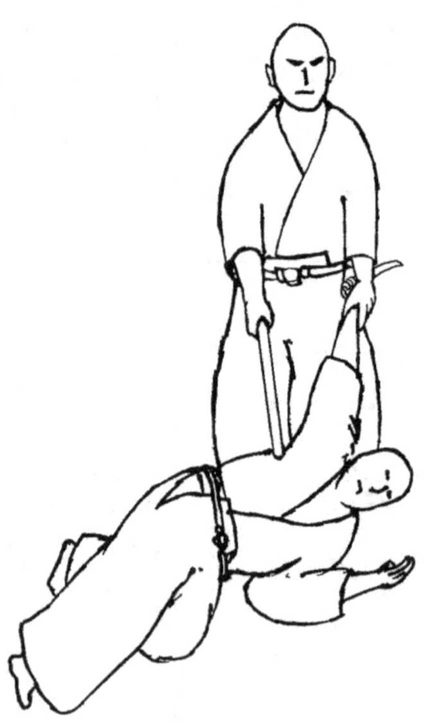

Nagare Dori
Flowing Capture

This technique begins the same as the previous one. The Attacker tries to stab you in the stomach with his short sword.
Respond by stepping to the right with your right foot and allowing your body to rotate counterclockwise. Grab your Attacker's right wrist with your left hand, since he is holding his short sword in that hand. Wedge one end of your Hanbo behind his hip, then push your right hand into the spot where his right arm meets his shoulder. With your left foot, step diagonally across to the right, behind the Attacker. Since you are holding his right wrist and the Hanbo is wedged between his hip and the spot where the arm meets the shoulder, his arm is in a Gyaku, or joint lock.

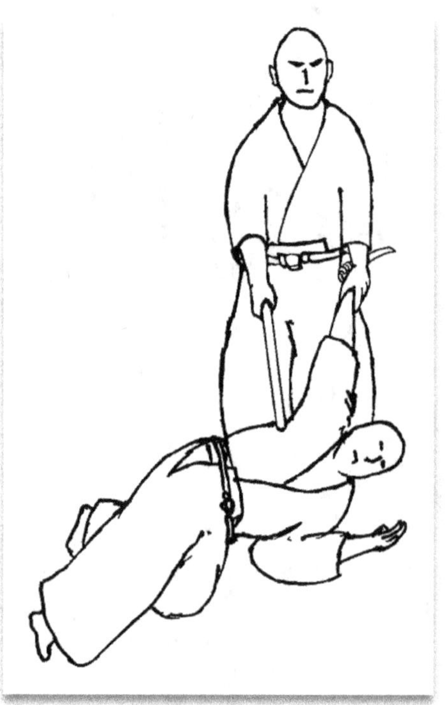

The Attacker will fall face-up on the ground. Use the Bo-jiri, butt of the stick, to strike Waki-tsubo, the vital point in the armpit.

霞掛

相手と相對し前にと念じくのにて戒腹部に突入り手る

戒左足左横一歩前き体を転じ右手にて敵の小刀持つ

右手商を握り左棒先を敵の

棒持つ左手を敵の右手ほろ付根の止に持って行き

右足を廻れ店に仲を転じる時は敵の右腕棒で逆押と

なる其ま、右足利き堅して押へ込み

行違

相手方も左戒り左互方行違ふ時敵は忽ちかくし以たる

小刀にて右横に戒れをちらんとす我れ左足一歩左へ体を

削って左手其ま、右手肩の度へ左横下にて小刃を度

ける同時に合一歩左足左へ斜に体を転じて左手放

ちて左棒先敵の宙部を打つ

霞掛

相手方、前と仝じく小刀にて我腹部に突入り来る。

我、左足左横一歩開き体を転じ右手にて敵の小刀持つ右手首を握り左棒先を敵の前下腹部を持って行き棒持つ左手を敵の右手後ろ付根の上に持って行き右足を廻れ右に体を転じる時は敵の右腕棒で逆押へとなる。其ま、右足引き坐して押へ込み。

行違

相手方も左、我も左、互方、行違ふ時、敵は忽ちかくし以ち（隠し持ち）たる小刀にて右横に我れを切らんとす。我れ左足一歩左へ体を開いて左手其ま、右手肩の處へ左横下にして小刀を受ける。同時に今一歩左足左へ斜

Kasumi Kake
Causing Mist

Kasumi Kake
Causing Mist

The Attacker attacks the same way as in the previous technique. He tries to stab you in the stomach with his short sword.

Respond by stepping to the left with your left foot and allowing your body to turn clockwise. The Attacker is holding his short sword in his right hand, so you seize the wrist of that hand with your right hand. With your left hand, plant the end of your Hanbo on the Attacker's lower abdomen.

Then push your left hand up into Tsukene, the point where his arm meets his shoulder. Swing your right foot back and to the right, rotating your body clockwise. This will cause the Hanbo to push into the back of his arm, locking it from the back as you hold his wrist.

Finally, pull your right foot back and drop onto your knee as you press the Hanbo down.

Yuki Chigai
Crossing Paths

You and your Attacker are walking towards each other, and it seems as if you will both pass on each other's left side. Suddenly, the Attacker draws a concealed short sword he was carrying and cuts to your right side.

Respond by taking a step to your left with your left foot, allowing your body to rotate clockwise. Keep your left hand in place as you raise your right hand so the Hanbo is level with your right shoulder. This means you will block the cut on your lower left side. Then immediately step diagonally to the left with your left foot and rotate your body clockwise. Release the Hanbo with you left hand swing the Hanbo around so the left end strikes your Attacker in the face.

額砕

相手が小刀我が腹部に突き来る

我左足一歩左へ上て体を転じ左棒の○と棒申真の虚に辷べらせて右棒を以って敵の小刀持つ小手打つ

左手放ち左棒之敵の顔面を打ち砕く

当返し

理方小刀大上段に切込まんとす

敵上のその進ち込みまるそく同じに我れ左足を引て左手放ち左棒之敵の水月に当込む

同じに我れ返り一歩右足前の道

坂落し

敵小刀我胸部に突アリ来る

我左足一歩左横前に立の道体を斜めにして左手右手は右側直直ぐに下にして肩の虚に持って行き右手は右側

敵の小刀受け同付に敵の右側から帰ろに飛び廻り

顔砕

相手方、小刀我が腹部に突き来る。

我左足一歩左へして体を転じ左棒の手を棒中真の處にすべらせて右棒先にて敵の小刀持つ小手打つ。左手放ち左棒先敵の顔面を打ち砕く。

当返し

相手方、小刀大上段に切込まんとす。

敵、一歩前進切込み来ると同じ（同時）に我も一歩右足前進左足坐し左手放ち左棒先敵の水月に当込む。

坂落し

敵、小刀我胸部に突入り来る。

我、左足一歩左横前に前進、体を斜めにして左手右手肩の處に持って行き、右手は右側真直ぐに下にして敵の小刀受け、

Kao Kudaki
Breaking the Face

The Attacker is armed with a short sword and attacks by trying to stab you in the stomach.

Respond by stepping out to the left with your left foot and allowing your body to rotate clockwise. Slide your left hand holding the left side of the Hanbo towards the center and strike the Attackers wrist, which is holding his short sword.

Release the Hanbo with your left hand and strike the Attacker in the face with the left end of the Hanbo, breaking his face.

Ategaeshi
Returning Strike

Your Attacker is armed with a short sword and cuts down from Daijodan, Upper Stance.

The moment your Attacker steps forward to cut, you also step forward with your right foot, immediately dropping down on your left knee. While doing this release your left hand and drive the left end of your Hanbo into the Attacker's Suigetsu, the solar plexus, with the left end of your Hanbo.

Saka Otoshi
Falling Down the Slope

The Attacker, armed with a short sword, tries to stab you in the chest.

Respond by stepping diagonally to the left with your left foot. As your body rotates clockwise, raise your left hand up to the height of your right shoulder. Drop your right hand straight down on your right side, blocking the Attacker's strike. Then immediately jump around his right side, so you end up behind him. Use your right hand to slide the Hanbo forward across his neck with your right hand, so that the end of the Hanbo, where you originally held with your left hand, extends out the other side. With your left hand gripping the Hanbo over his right shoulder, grab the left end of the Hanbo with your right hand from behind. Drop your hips and, with the Hanbo across his throat, do a Sei-oi Nage, Back Throw.

左手棒の中真まですべらして左手放ち左手構之

敵の左肩より面に廻し再び左手にて敵の右肩に

出し棒を握り一寸腰をそれて棒で面━━めて

ゐろから脊頂に投げ坂落(

中段型

中段型は棒慈の構ゑ横びみる

相手方大刀大上段我れは右手棒状にして左へすり

敵大刀我面上より切込み来る我右足右側に一歩開き

ハ手返

て体一転じ棒のま、棒を振て敵のみ手打ち砕く

逆落

相手方前と仝じく我れも亦前通り

敵大刀我頭上に切込み来る我左足一歩左へ開き

左手棒の中真まで、すべらして左手放ち左手棒先敵の左肩より首に廻し、再び左手にて敵の右肩に出た棒先握り、一寸腰を入れて棒で首しめて後ろから背負い投げ坂落し。

中段型

中段型は棒無心の構無構である。

小手返

相手方、大刀大上段。我は右手棒杖にしたる姿なり。
敵大刀、我面上より切込み来る。我、右足右側に一歩開きて体を転じ、其のま、棒を振って敵の小手打ち砕く。

逆落

相手方、前と全じく我れも前通り。
敵大刀、我頭上に切込み来る。我、左足一歩左へ開き

Chudan Gata
Mid-Level Techniques

The Mid-Level Techniques are all from Mushin no Kamae, Mu Kamae, Without Mind Stance, No-Stance.

- *Mushin Kamae Mu Kamae*
  Without Mind, No-stance

Kotegaeshi
Reverse Wrist Strike

The Attacker is armed with a Tachi, long sword, and is in Daijodan, Upper Stance. You are standing with the Hanbo in your right hand as if you are holding a walking stick. Your Attacker cuts to the top of your head with his long sword.

Respond by stepping to the right with your right foot and allow your body to rotate counterclockwise. Continue the turn and swing your Hanbo so you strike and break the Attacker's wrists

Gyaku Otoshi
Reverse Drop

The Attacker is armed the same way as in the previous technique and attacks the same way. You also move the same.
The Attacker cuts down with his long sword to the top of your head. Step out to the left with your left foot. At the same time use your right hand to spin the left end of your Hanbo around to strike the Attacker in the right side of the face.

同時に右手棒左廻—にて敵の横面を打つ

掛技
相手方大刀大立度己に切込まんとす一歩交えに敵
の左リ裏を左廻—にて打込み小手を廻って
左廻—にて敵の右面を打砕く

外輪
相手方大刀眼眠より変化—て突込み来る
我れ右足一歩右側に開きて棒を右廻—にて敵
の二の腕を打込んで左手持ち柔へ水月に突入る

奥
虜
一刀
相手方大刀大立度切込み来る 我右足右側に一歩開き
て左足堅—て左手放を棒—下がり繰廻—小手打砕

同時に右手棒左廻しにて敵の横面を打つ。

拂技

相手方、大刀大上段正に切込まんとす。一歩先に敵の左小手裏を左廻しにて打込み小手を廻して左廻しにて敵の右面を打碎く。

外輪

相手方、大刀晴眼より変化して突込み来る。我れ右足一歩右側に開きて棒を右廻しにて敵の二の腕を打ち込んで左手持ち添へ水月に突入る。

奥傳

一刀

相手方、大刀大上段、切込み来る。我、右足右側に一歩開きて左足坐して左手放ち棒下から繰廻し小手內卒

Harai Waza
Sweeping Technique

The Attacker is armed with a Tachi, long sword, and cuts straight down from Daijodan, upper stance.
Respond by stepping directly towards the Attacker and swinging the Hanbo up to the left, striking him on the underside of his left wrist. Rotate your wrist to the left and use the left swing to strike the Attacker in the right side of his face, breaking it.

Sotowa
Outer Ring

The Attacker, armed with a Tachi, long sword, switches to Seigan Kamae, a mid-level stance, and suddenly stabs forward.[8]
Respond by stepping out to the right with your right foot. Rotate the Hanbo up and around to the right and strike the Attacker in Ni-no-ude, the bicep. Then join your left hand on the Hanbo and stab to Suigetsu, the solar plexus.

Itto
One Cut

The Attacker is standing in Daijodan with a Tachi, long sword. When he cuts down take one step out to the right with your right foot and drop down onto your left knee. Release the Hanbo with your left hand and spin it from below to strike Kote Uchi Kudaki, Breaking the Insides of the Wrists.

---

[8] This means your opponent first seems to be readying to attack from an upper stance, but then suddenly shifts to a middle stance and stabs forward.

返倒

前の通り拳下から繰廻し小手打砕返て通す棒にて敵左足中関節打を砕を

跳落し

相手刀を上段又刀切込み来る
我一歩の左足左横に開りて右手揆そのま、小手廻右肩から出して敵の両腕中関節打砕を
「此の挙を後ろに持たるま、小手廻」とそふ事は此の字通り右左も自由百花です一二手程の稽習がかる程どは大刀を意合抜き自由である之が出来得ねば大刀を

股掛け

相手方から同じく大刀上段切込み来る左足左側へ一步開って其のま、右手小手廻して下から上へ敵

返倒

　前の通り

棒下から繰廻し小手打碎きて通す棒にて敵左足中関節打ち碎く。

跳落し

相手方、大上段大刀切込み来る。

我、一歩左足左横に開いて右手棒そのまゝ、小手廻し右肩から出して敵の両腕中関節打碎く。

（此の棒をわがすぁわ後ろに持ちたるまゝ小手返しと云ふ事は、一ヶ年程の練習がいる。私などは此の小手返し右左とも自由自在ですが、之が出来得れば大刀でも意合抜きも自由である。）

相手方、前と司じく大刀大上段切込み来る。左足左側へ一

Kaeshi Taoshi
Returning Knockdown

This technique begins the same way as the previous one.
Swing your Hanbo up from below and around to strike and break the Attacker's wrist. Then strike the Attacker's left knee, breaking it.

Tobi Otoshi
Jumping and Falling

The Attacker, armed with a Tachi, long sword, cuts down from Daijodan, upper stance.
Respond by stepping to your left with your left foot and allowing your body to rotate clockwise. Keeping your right hand on the Hanbo, rotate it behind your back and up so it sticks out from your right shoulder. Then strike the Attacker across the top of both elbows, breaking them.
(Rotating the Hanbo behind your back like this, without letting go of it is called Kotegaeshi, or Reversing the Wrist. It takes almost a year of training to master. I and others have become able to do Kotegaeshi freely and without hesitation on both the left and right sides. If you become adept at this, you will become able to draw a Tachi with great rapidity and immediately strike your Attacker.)

Mata Kake
Attacking the Groin

As in the previous technique your Attacker cuts down from Daijodan with a Tachi.
Respond by stepping to the side with your left foot. From there do a Kotegaeshi with your right hand and strike the Attacker's wrists from below. Then immediately rotate your wrist and strike a rising blow to the Attacker's groin.

の小手打立る同時に再びい手を返して敵の股を打砕
る下股斬り

小手拂

横に開くりと同時に棒そのまゝ小手返して右手右
肩より棒、勢いらて敵の両小手打込て小手返し
顔面打砕く

相手の刀睛眼青化て突入り来る貳左足一歩左

以上

天押雲命三十八代後裔

熱田房綱寺

延元三年五月三十日楠正成名和長年と共に官軍六
味方す敵将上杉伊豆守畠山修理太夫足利尾張守

の小手打上る。同時に再び小手を返して敵の股を打上げる下段掛け。

小手拂

　相手方、大刀晴眼変化して突入り来る。我、左足一歩左横に開くのと同時に棒そのまゝ小手返しして右手右肩より棒、勢い良く敵の両小手打込み小手返し顔面に打砕く。以上

手押雲命三十八代後裔

熱田房綱秀

ノート

。敵将上杉伊豆守、畠山修理大夫、足利尾張守

延元三年正月二十七日、楠正成、名和長年と共に官軍に御味方す

手押雲命…天押雲根命（あめのおしくもねのみこと）。別名、天村雲命（あめのむらくものみこと）、天二上命（あめのふたがみのみこと）、後小橋命（のちおばせのみこと）。

延元三年正月二十七日…正確には、延元元年（建武三年）正月二十七日の京都四条河原の戦いの事と思われる。

Kote Harai
Wrist Sweep

Your Attacker is armed with a Tachi, long sword, and suddenly switches to standing in Seigan, clear-eyed, a mid-level stance, and stabs forward.

Respond by stepping out to the left with your left foot and allowing your body to rotate clockwise. At the same time, do right Kotegaeshi, rotating the Hanbo behind your back so the right end sticks out behind your right shoulder. Then strike across both the Attacker's wrists with great power before rotating the Hanbo around and striking him in the face, breaking it.

End

Transmitted to Atsuda Bo Tsunahide
38th descendant of Ameno Oshi Kumo no Mikoto[9]

---

[9] This deity is also known as Ameno Oshi Kumonenomikoto, Amenomurakumo no Mikoto, Amenofutagami no Mikoto as well as Nochiobase no Mikoto.

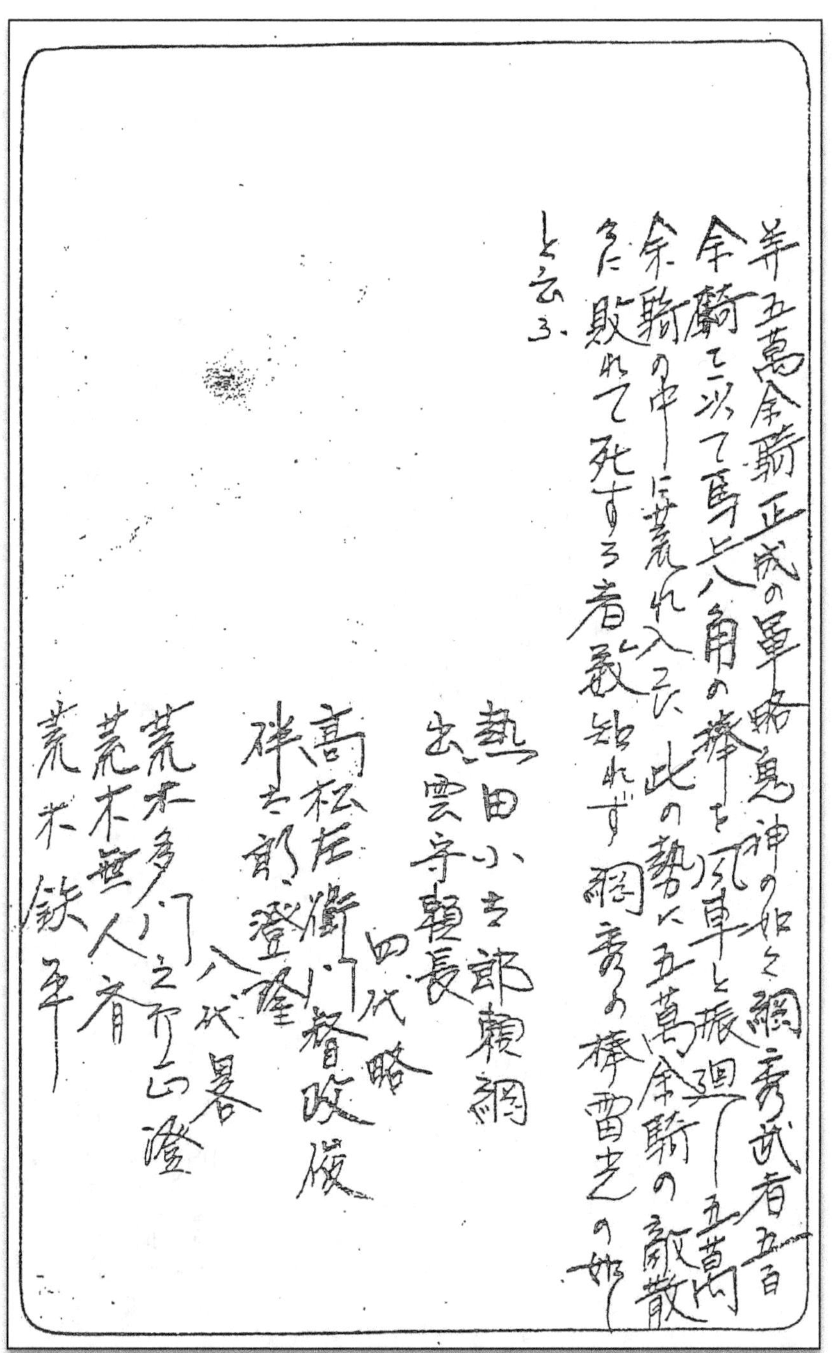
彗五萬余騎正成の軍略鳥神の如く網秀武者五百
余騎を以て馬と人角の輩を兵車と振迴一五萬
余騎の中に荒れ入てん此の勢に五萬余騎の潰散
を敗れて死する者教知れず網秀の棒雷芝の如
と云ふ

熱田小文部療網
出雲守頼長　四代略
高松左衛ハ督改侵
伴吉郎登崖　八代暴澄
荒木多八門之丁正澄
荒木無人有
荒木鉄平

等五萬余騎。正成の軍略、鬼神の如く。綱秀、武者五百余騎を以って馬上八角の棒を風車と振廻し、五萬余騎の中に荒れ入った。此の勢に五萬余騎の敵、散々に敗れて死する者数知れず。綱秀の棒、雷光の如しと云ふ。

熱田小太郎頼綱

出雲守頼長

　　四代略

高松左衛門督政俊

伴太郎澄隆

　　八代畧

荒木多門之介正澄

荒木無人斉

荒木鉄平

On January 27th in the 3rd year of Engen (1338[10]) Atsuda was serving the imperial army alongside Kusonooki Masashige and Nawa Nagatoshi. The opposing forces lead by Uesugi Guardian of Izu, [11] Hatakeyam Shuridayu, [12] Ashikaga Guardian of Owari. [13] ……had over 50,000 mounted Samurai. Masashige's military strategy was as clever as if it had been designed by a fierce god set on destruction.

Hidetsune lead a group of 500 mounted Samurai, each armed with an 8-sided staff. They charged into the midst of the 50,000 mounted Samurai and swinging their weapons like windmills. The 50,000 Samurai reeled away from the onslaught and fled in confusion, leaving untold dead. It is said Hidetsuna swung his staff like a flash of lightning.

- Atsuda Kotaro Yoritsune
- Guardian of Izumo Norinaga
- Four Generations abbreviated
- Takamatsu Saemon [unknown]
- Bantaro Kiyotaka
- Eight Generations Abbreviated
- Araki Tamonnosuke Masakiyo
- Araki Mujinsai
- Araki Teppei

---

[10] This seems to be describing the Battle of Minatogawa which took place in Hyogo Prefecture in 1336. The illustrations on the back cover show this battle.

[11] This is referring to Uesugi Norifusa 上杉憲房 who died in this battle.

[12] This is referring to Hatakeyama Kunikiyo 畠山国清

[13] This is referring to Shiba Takatsune 斯波高経 who was also known as Ashikaga Takatsune 足利高経.

Translator's Note:
This is the section of the Kojiki *Records of Ancient Matters* that mentions the origin of Hanbo. The Kojiki was written in the 8th century and contains the mythology and royal lineage of early Japan. Motoori Norinaga, an Era author of an annotated version of the Kojiki published in 1754 felt the work was,
A true account of actual events that when read correctly, could reveal Japan in its pristine, ideal state as a community where the kami, the emperor and the people lived in harmony

The Kojiki
Translated by B.H. Chamberlain (1882)
The Nether Distant Land

The deity Great-House-Prince spoke to him, saying: Thou must set off to the Nether-Distant-Land where dwells His Impetuous-Male-Augustness. That great deity will certainly counsel thee." So on his obeying her commands and arriving at the august place of His Impetuous-Male-Augustness, the latter's daughter the Forward-Princess came out, and saw him, and they exchanged glances and were married, and she went in again, and told her father, saying: " A very beautiful deity has come." Then the great deity went out and looked, and said: " This is the Ugly-Male-Deity-of-the-Reed-Plains," and at once calling him in, made him sleep in the snake-house. Hereupon his wife, Her Augustness the Forward-Princess, gave her husband a snake-scarf, saying: " When the snakes are about to bite thee, drive them away by waving this scarf thrice."

So, on his doing as she bad instructed, the snakes became quiet, so that he came forth after calm slumbers. Again on the night of the next day the Impetuous--Male deity put him into the centipede and wasp-house; but as she again gave him a centipede and wasp-scarf, and instructed him as before, he came forth calmly.

Again the Impetuous-Male deity shot a whizzing barb into the middle of a large moor, and sent him to fetch the arrow, and, when be bad entered the moor, at once set fire to the moor all round. Thereupon, while he stood knowing no place of exit, a mouse came and said: " The inside is hollow-hollow; the outside is narrow-narrow." Owing to its speaking thus, he trod on the place, whereupon he fell in and hid himself, during which time

the fire burned past. Then the mouse brought out in its mouth and presented to him the whizzing barb. The feathers of the arrow were brought in their mouths by all the mouse's children.

Hereupon his wife the Forward-Princess came bearing mourning implements, and crying. Her father the great deity, thinking that the deity Great-Name-Possessor was already dead and done for, went out and stood on the moor, whereupon the deity Great-Name-Possessor brought the arrow and presented it to him, upon which the great deity, taking him into the house and calling him into an eight-foot spaced large room, made him take the lice off his head. So, on looking at the head, be saw that there were many centipedes there. Thereupon, as his wife gave to her husband berries of the muku tree and red earth, he chewed the berries to pieces, and spat them out with the red earth which he held in his mouth, so that the great deity believed him to be chewing up and spitting out the centipedes, and, feeling fond of him in his heart, fell asleep. Then the deity Great-Name-Possessor, grasping the great deity's hair, tied it fast to the various rafters of the house, and, blocking up the floor of the house with a five-hundred draught rock, and taking his wife the Forward-Princess on his back, then carried off the great deity's great life-sword and life-bow-and-arrows, as also his heavenly speaking-lute, and ran out.

But the heavenly speaking-lute brushed against a tree, and the earth resounded. So the great deity, who was sleeping, started at the sound, and pulled down the house. But while he was disentangling his hair which was tied to the rafters, the deity Great-Name-Possessor fled a long way.

So then, pursuing after him to the Even-Pass-of-Hades, and gazing on him from afar, be called out to the deity Great-Name-Possessor, saying: "With the great life-sword and the life-bow-and-arrows which thou carries, pursue thy half-brethren till they crouch on the august slopes of the passes, and pursue them till they are swept into the reaches of the rivers, and do thou, wretch! become the deity Master-of-the-Great-Land; and moreover, becoming the deity Spirit-of-the-Living-Land, and making my daughter the Forward-Princess thy consort, do thou make stout the temple-pillars at the foot of Mount Uka in the nethermost rock-bottom, and make high the crossbeams to the Plain-of-High-Heaven, and dwell there, thou villain!

So when, bearing the great sword and bow, he pursued and scattered the eighty deities, he did pursue them till they crouched on the august slope of every pass, he did pursue them till they were swept into every river, and then he began to make the land.